4 50

D1559339

NOTABLE
PERSONALITIES
AND
THEIR FAITH

NOTABLE PERSONALITIES AND THEIR FAITH

Compiled by Claude A. Frazier, M.D.

Library of Congress Catalog Card No. 72-89607
ISBN-0-8309-0083-7

Printed in the United States of America
By Independence Press, Independence, Missouri

DEDICATION

This book is dedicated to Dr. Robert Crouch who exemplified its spirit. His faith was evident to those around him throughout his terminal illness.

ACKNOWLEDGMENT

I would like to extend my sincere appreciation to the contributors to this book.

I want to thank Mr. Luther Thigpen, executive editor of the *Asheville Citizen-Times* newspaper, who printed these testimonies as a weekly feature.

In addition, I am grateful to my wife, Kay, and to my former secretary, Miss Carolyn Baxter, for their work in the organization of this feature.

I would also like to thank my secretary, Miss Nancy Beyer, for her assistance with the final compiling of the manuscript.

CONTENTS

PREFACE

The public is always interested in the religious beliefs of famous personalities. When a man tells us what he believes he is at the same time telling us what he doesn't believe. He provides us with an opportunity to weigh his insights against our own and to accept or reject what he has to say.

This collection is quite diverse but it does include statements of representatives from many different backgrounds. Some of these people indicate cultic antecedents; others are from theologically orthodox homes and churches. Some have articulated their convictions in nontheological and general terms; some are long and some are short on biblical content. But all of the authors give us helpful insights into what they believe, and this enables us to understand and evaluate them more fairly.

Harold Lindsell
Editor
Christianity Today

INTRODUCTION

Shortly after we become acquainted with someone, we learn of his occupation, his hobbies, his likes and dislikes, and his political affiliations. Apparently, these are easy subjects about which to talk. But rarely do we know of a person's religious faith, his inner thoughts and feelings concerning his beliefs and trust in God.

It is my personal opinion that if a person has any strong beliefs, religious or otherwise, other people will know of these. In the realm of faith, a person who has a deep faith is not only willing to share it but wants to share it. Only by sharing is he able to help others.

Many great personalities were contacted about discussing their faith, but only a few responded. I feel that those who did respond truly have a strong faith and I greatly appreciate their willingness to share this faith with others.

The contributors to *Notable Personalities and Their Faith* have exemplified James 2:17, "So faith by itself, if it has no works, is dead." Not only have they shared their faith but they have also shared the fruit of their works with others.

It is my sincere wish that this book will strengthen and influence others to have a deeper faith in God and to be willing to express this faith in words and action to other people.

AMERICA SEEKS THE BLESSING OF GOD

By Richard M. Nixon
President of the United States

John Adams was the first President to live in the executive residence we call the White House. His first night there he wrote a letter to his wife, Abigail, in which he said: "Before I end my letter, I pray Heaven to bestow the best of blessings on this house and all that shall hereafter inhabit it. May none but wise and honest men ever rule under this roof."

Prayer knows no boundary of time; we in America today, in the spirit of Adams, seek the blessing of God on our nation and its leaders.

At a time in our nation's history when the power of prayer is needed more than ever, it is fitting that we publicly demonstrate our faith in the power of prayer.

I am especially reminded of Benjamin Franklin's immortal thought when he remarked that if no sparrow can fall to the ground without God's notice, no nation can rise from the ground without his help. Throughout our history despairing men and women have found sustaining solace in the word of God as written in the Bible. Families have been guided by its enlightened precepts. Statesmen and leaders have drawn inspiration from its teachings, and courage from the enriching experience it records.

13

It is unique among books and treasured by men and nations. The power of the universal truths it holds is appropriately refreshed within our hearts. The past has proved that we have much to gain by our devotion to the scriptures. The future holds great promise if we heed past lessons well.

All of our Presidents did not have the same degree of religious faith. They did not belong to the same church and, for some, religious faith was a deeper, different experience than for others.

Yet each one, whether he was a churchgoer or not, recognized in the awesome position of the power of the Presidency the necessity for divine guidance. Each recognized the fact that this nation is a nation under God, and that from the beginning it has had a spiritual strength far more important than the enormous economic potential that has been developed or the military strength that it has possessed.

Regardless of our background, regardless of our religious denominations, all of us in positions of leadership have recognized, in varying degrees, that this is a nation which has had a spiritual value upon which we have relied.

We must pray as if everything depended upon God, recognizing that America is a nation under God.

RELIGION AND POLITICS

By George McGovern
Senator from South Dakota
and 1972 Presidential Candidate

English author Hilaire Belloc was once told by the chairman of a public meeting that he could address the audience on any subject except religion and politics.

"Whereupon," said Belloc, "having been prevented from discussing either of the subjects that most concerned mankind, I turned on my heel and departed."

If one believes that avoiding controversy is essential to the good life, he will tend to support the chairman's ruling. But if he believes that each individual has some responsibility for the spiritual and political health of the community, he will endorse Belloc's position.

I have no doubt that the Christian bears a special responsibility for both the spiritual vitality and the political tone of his society. It is unthinkable for him to be indifferent to such important issues as education, social justice, public health, the conservation of resources, and peace or war. Indeed, the preamble of the Constitution places on each citizen the responsibility "to establish justice, insure domestic tranquility, provide for the common defense, promote the general welfare, and secure the blessings of liberty. . . ."

Those great issues of citizenship were spelled out by men who drew deeply on their religious heritage, and at bottom such matters involve ethical and spiritual judgments. This is not to say that every Christian should be a candidate for public office, although that is a calling many Christians have heard in the past and need to hear in the future. What is required of all Christians, however, is an obligation to think soberly and exercise judgment about public issues, candidates, and programs as effectively as possible. This means not only voting but also influencing the quality and the direction of our political process.

The Christian has much to contribute by mixing in politics. Where there is a tendency toward narrow, partisan expediency, he can help keep the eyes of the community focused on the larger problems of our society.

When appeals to passion and prejudice are rife, he can counter with the voice of reason.

Where there is bitterness or violence, he can exercise the restraining influence of charity and good humor.

Where there is a laxity or indifference in the face of dishonesty, he can bring to bear the demands of a Christian conscience.

At a time when nuclear energy has erased whatever claim warfare might once have offered as a means of settling international disputes, the Christian can help reassert the claims of brotherhood and the family of man.

FROM RICHES TO RICHER

By J.C. Penney
Founder of J.C. Penney Company, Inc.

One night late in 1931, I was convinced I would never see another dawn. I wrote farewell letters to my family. Then I waited for the end—a failure at the age of fifty-six.

I was in a sanitarium at Battle Creek, Michigan, a nervous and physical wreck, plagued by shingles, and certain I did not have a friend on earth. I believed the whole world was against me, including my wife and children.

As a result of the financial dislocations of the depression, I had watched the fruits of a lifetime of toil swept away in a few brief months—a fortune estimated at $40,000,000. This included all of my stock in the J.C. Penney Company, an organization I had seen grow from a single small Wyoming store in 1902 to the world's largest department store chain, with modern merchandising centers in every state in the Union.

From being in a position to move mountains (I thought), I was overnight transformed into just another beaten man, in late middle age, flat broke, and with no apparent future. As is not unusual in such crackups, I blamed everyone except myself. My failure seemed to weigh a ton on my shoulders.

Somehow that dreadful night passed. The next morning as I shuffled from my room I heard the sound of singing coming from the mezzanine. The song was a hymn. I will never forget the title. It was "God Will Take Care of You." I was drawn to the source of the song. A group of patients were holding a prayer meeting. Wearily I joined them.

I prayed for God to take care of me, and an amazing thing happened. Suddenly I knew that he would. A profound sense of inner release came over me. The heavy weight seemed lifted from my spirit. That moment marked a turning point in my life.

Perhaps the facing of impending death was a sign that a new man was being born in me. Or maybe at long last I was learning how to pray, by truly submitting myself to the will of God.

It had never occurred to me that I did not know how to pray. I regarded myself as a religious man. My father, who supported his family with a farm near Hamilton, Missouri, had been a minister in the old-fashioned Primitive Baptist Church. He reared me in the strict discipline of that faith. In all my dealings I had sought to follow the principle of the Golden Rule.

But I hadn't realized what had taken place in me. As I rose in wealth and power, dealing in millions of dollars and guiding the activities of thousands of men, I had grown to depend entirely upon my own judgment. My spiritual life had been stored away in a separate compartment. God had very little hand in my everyday thinking. With this condition prevailing, in the matter of prayer I was as helpless as a man in deep water who doesn't know how to swim.

In any case, a remarkable change followed that session of prayer. I rapidly regained my mental and bodily health. Within a couple of months I was well enough to return to my family. We had been living on our sixty-five-acre estate at White Plains, New York, in a manner commensurate with

22

wealth that no longer existed. Now, with my wife, I had the strength to take the steps that were needed.

Our children, two daughters and a son, were sent to live with their grandmother in Phoenix, Arizona, until things got better. We discharged the servants and closed down the large house, except for the kitchen and one bedroom, creating an apartment my wife could manage alone. We laid up our expensive automobile.

The J. C. Penney Company offered to put me on a salary. It had always been one of my proudest boasts that I had never drawn a cent of pay for my services to the company. But with my stockholdings gone, such pride was out of the question. I had to get on a payroll if my family was to continue to eat. I gratefully accepted the offer and plunged into work.

The years that followed were not easy. But two of the banks with which I had done business agreed not to close out my holdings entirely. This gave me a small foothold for the long climb back. But I still had many inner obstacles to overcome. However, when things got too bad, I drew strength from a piece of paper I carried with me always. On it I had copied these words from the Ninety-first Psalm:

"He shall cover thee with his feathers, and under his wings shalt thou trust: His truth shall be thy shield and buckler."

And I prayed, developing the habit of spending fifteen to thirty minutes in prayer and meditation just before retiring so that my last thoughts before going to sleep were on God and my spiritual needs.

In time I got back on firm ground. I had much less in a material sense than before, but I had gained immeasurably in spiritual wealth, something that cannot be calculated in dollars and cents. I had finally turned to God for guidance in all the acts and decisions of my life.

MY FAITH AND WHAT IT MEANS TO ME

By Maria Beale Fletcher
Miss America 1962

The word *faith* implies, to me at least, a deeper and perhaps more intangible meaning than the word *belief,* though the two words are closely related. One believes, I think, with his brain; by that I mean the thinking, analyzing, calculating part of his brain. But faith dwells in the deeper crevices of one's makeup. It has its home in the subconscious mind. It is a part of one's soul. Faith in God as the Supreme Creator of all the universe—the stars in the heavens, the life in the seas, and all the life on the land—and faith that this Supreme Being loves us, cares for us, and has given us the miracle of life touches our souls with a sense of constant well-being. Faith springs from our inner self and, moving outward through our physical makeup, gives us confidence and a feeling of serenity even during those moments when the surface scratches of everyday living are somewhat degrading.

We read the newspapers, listen to the radio, and look at television—then conclude that we who inhabit the planet Earth at this particular moment in history are heading full speed down the path that leads to utter chaos, death, and destruction. But the faith that dwells within says, "I am a child of God. I am a part of the universe. A part of me is locked up in the bosom of God and can never die."

25

I believe that the discoveries of science, the medical profession, and the knowledge gained from our exploration of space will greatly improve our lot upon this earth. I believe in evolution of the species, and I believe there is an evolution of man's spiritual nature. It took us centuries to realize that slavery is wrong and cannot be tolerated. Someday I believe we will realize that war is wrong and cannot be tolerated. Man has finally realized that life—all life—is important to all other life on this earth. I have faith that our environment will be restored to a health-giving condition. We are now keenly aware of the problem, and that is the first step toward rectifying it.

I believe that the same God who created the stars a million billion light-years away also created the plant that grows outside my window and the baby that coos so joyously in the crib beside me. The aged debate as to whether Darwin's theory of evolution of the species conflicts with the Bible's account of the creation of the universe is, to my way of thinking, a foolish waste of time. Man cannot begin to understand time, so what difference does the time element make in regard to the creation of the universe?

Man can exist without faith, but I do not believe he can live joyously without faith. Faith needs feeding and nourishing, just as a plant needs feeding and nourishing. How? It is nourished by prayer, in which one communes with God; by meditation, in which one listens to God; by walking to the high mountain peaks where one can see the glory of God, and there, while facing the morning sun, feel the joy of God upon all the land; by reading inspirational books of poetry, philosophy, religion, the Bible, and coming into contact with others who have felt God's presence in their lives.

Faith brings meaning and happiness to our lives. Joy replaces all forms of despair. We know that God knows just how the universe is unfolding and revealing itself, and all is well. With faith in our hearts we can close our eyes and say, "I am at peace with myself. I am at peace with God."

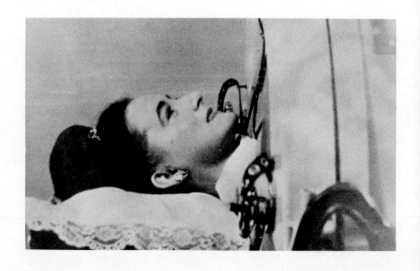

PRISONER FOR LIFE

By Katherine Bryson
Victim of Paralysis

"I'll be home for Christmas"—that was the message I told my parents to give to my four children. They had not been permitted to visit me in the hospital.

It all began August 26, 1950. I was twenty-four years old and expecting my fourth child. For two days I had been ill with a sore throat, stiff neck, and high fever. My doctor was called and I was admitted to the hospital; there my spine was tapped and I was given the terrifying diagnosis—poliomyelitis. I was overwhelmed by this news. I tried not to show my emotions but all I could think of was death and God. I was transferred to an orthopedic hospital. But nothing could penetrate the thoughts that were running through my mind about dying and meeting God.

I wondered about my conversion in that little country church at the age of ten. I questioned if I really had made a strong enough commitment to Jesus Christ, because during the years that followed I felt that I had not lived a better life than anyone else. I didn't receive any help from God about my burdened heart or my physical pain. I was in critical condition, both physically and spiritually, and the baby was on its way.

That night nurses and doctors sped noiselessly and efficiently about the room talking in anxious whispers. Would I be able to bear my child even though I was becoming paralyzed? I was so fearful, so sick, and bewildered. The midsummer heat was stifling as the dramatic scene played itself out in the quiet of the room.

A muffled cry caused a sense of relief to course through the room, dispelling the suspense that had settled over its occupants. As the first rays of the early morning sun reached through the blinds, the announcement "It's a girl!" rang out joyously.

By the time the baby was delivered, I was completely paralyzed from my neck down and was immediately confined to an iron lung. The iron lung was a perfect prison system. As its prisoner I was totally subjected to it for the purpose of breathing. I felt as if I had completely lost my rights as an independent individual.

"Let the sighing of the prisoner come before thee; according to the greatness of thy power preserve thou those that are appointed to die."

During the nine months I stayed in the hospital it was a battle to stay alive—the will was weak and all hope gone. It seemed that I could not get through to God. I loved him, but I felt that God had let me down when I needed him most. The days were especially dark because I could get no relief. My mother read to me from the Bible each day and I became especially interested in the scriptures that tell of divine healing. One of my favorites was, "And with his stripes we are healed." Also, I appreciated, "Have mercy upon me, O Lord; for I am weak: O Lord, heal me; for my bones are vexed." I prayed that the Lord would heal me completely, if it was his will. Many people—people of many faiths—were praying for my recovery, and of course it goes without saying that my mother was always faithful.

A minister of the gospel prayed for me and anointed my head. My little children—Philip, who was six years of age; Langdon, three and one-half; and David, two and one-half—sent messages to me that they prayed to Jesus every night to make their mother well and let her come home again. (The baby Karen was healthy and strong and was cared for at another local hospital.) It touched my heart to know that so many people were praying for me.

I have now been in the iron lung for twenty-two years, twenty-four hours a day, and I am still completely paralyzed.

My physical condition has not changed; however, the Lord has given me his power to live above my circumstances. He has enabled me to accept my illness as his divine will. At times I have to pray for grace for just five minutes longer. God has been gracious to me. He saved my life and permitted me to see my children grow up, and I purposed in my heart to be content with whatever the Lord has planned for me. "I can do all things through Christ which strengtheneth me."

Jesus Christ has become very real to me. Without his love, grace, and mercy I could not have tolerated my life in this condition. I do not think now it is the Lord's will to heal me. However, I do feel that the scriptures I read on healing helped me spiritually because I have the will to live—and I hope, and even dream.

I think God has a purpose in my life and I believe I am following his pattern for my life.

"And we know that all things work together for good to them that love God, to them who are the called according to his purpose."

Oh, yes—I was home for Christmas that year. I kept my promise to my children.

GOD HAS BEEN KIND TO AMERICA

By George Romney
Secretary of Housing and
Urban Development

God has dealt kindly with Americans. He placed us on this great continent, and made us stewards of its vast resources and its beauty. Here we grew and prospered, sheltered by great natural barriers from much of the turmoil, threat, and strife which plagues less favored lands and peoples.

I believe that the hand of the Creator guided the formation and development of our country.

I believe that the Declaration of Independence and the Constitution of the United States are divinely inspired documents, written by men especially raised up by their Creator for that purpose. I believe that God has made and preserved us as a nation, for a purpose—that the practice of our inspired principles may one day bring freedom to all mankind.

What are these principles?

They are old and familiar, but they are also new and fresh: the authority of the Creator; the right to worship according to the dictates of our own conscience; the separation of church and state; the sanctity of the individual; the brotherhood of man; the state as servant and creature of man; the dispersion of social, political, and economic power that freedom may be insured; the assurance that men should compete

33

and cooperate and be rewarded on the basis of what they contribute to society.

These principles have served us well. Upon our spiritual foundation, we have built unique political, social, and economic institutions which have released the God-given potential of more people than ever in history.

This land is choice above all other lands. It is given to us in trust, and I believe no people will continue to inhabit it in freedom who do not seek to know and do the will of God.

I believe this nation, which Lincoln called an "almost chosen people," was put upon this earth for a purpose—to help lift the burdens of tyranny and want that one day all may be free.

We must ponder in our prayers what contribution we can make to the renewal of our nation. There are enough decent, courageous people in this country to reshape private and public life almost overnight, if they would throw themselves into the task. I join in praying that God will send us men and women equal to the time in which we live.

It will not be easy. But we are not alone. We have God's promise through Isaiah:

> "He giveth power to the faint; and to them that have strength. . . . They that wait upon the Lord shall renew their strength; they shall mount up with wings as eagles; they shall run, and not be weary; and they shall walk, and not faint."

GOALS
IN THE GAME
OF LIFE

By Tom Landry

Coach of the Dallas Cowboys

It is a little difficult at times to give a personal testimony because it is personal—this relationship with the Lord and Savior, Jesus Christ. But the wonderful thing one discovers is that it isn't necessary to be articulate or eloquent to express oneself about this relationship, because it is such a wonderful experience.

As I look back through the years, I can see now that the thing that was urging me on during my younger days was a desire to find Jesus Christ. I believe the Holy Spirit is present in every one of us, and he is urging us to accept Christ as our Savior. Of course we have to knock, and the door will be opened for us to come in.

I was reared in the small town of Mission, located in the Rio Grande Valley. Mission had a population of 6,000, and I lived not unlike many young people live today. I went to Sunday school every Sunday, to church, and youth fellowship meetings. My dad was superintendent of the Sunday school. The thing that I remember most about those days was that I really couldn't separate Sunday from any other day of the week. I started my week on Monday, went to school through Friday, on Saturday I went to the movie, and on Sunday I went to church because everyone went to church on Sunday. But Sunday had no more significance for me than any other day. I was much more concerned with what was happening to Tom Mix or Hopalong Cassidy at the local movie theatre. But there was a gnawing feeling inside me all my life, urging me to reach some distant goal. I was seeking fulfillment and happiness materially.

Football was my whole world. Someone once defined religion as the total response to that which one feels is most valuable in his life. Really, my whole life revolved around football. I thought that if I could play on the team as a high school football player, win the championship, and all-district honors, this would be the fulfillment of all my dreams. As a team we did this my senior year. We went undefeated. We won in our region which covered the area from San Antonio to the Rio Grande Valley. We were scored on only once by a penalty. We won the championship by a score of 34 to 0, and I did make all-district halfback. The thing that surprised me most when it was over was that this feeling was still with me—the feeling that I had to do something else. I had not stilled this inner unrest.

I thought to myself that if I could go to college I would find fulfillment. I was a small-town boy; I had not been out of the valley very many times, yet I was somewhat sought after as a football player. I went to the University of Texas, and I felt that if I could just make the varsity team and be successful there I would fulfill all my dreams. I did make the varsity at the university, and still this inner feeling was not satisfied. I was fortunate enough to be captain of the University of Texas team. We won in the Sugar Bowl against Alabama; we won in the Orange Bowl against Georgia—all the things that one could hope to accomplish as an athlete—and yet this still wasn't enough.

I thought my niche in life must be professional football. I was fortunate enough to be drafted and I went on into professional football. I played with the New York Yankees one year before the All-American Conference joined the National Football League, and then I went with the New York Giants. I played and coached for the Giants ten years. During that time I was still setting goals, trying to satisfy this inner drive. I wanted to be on the all-pro team, which I was fortunate enough to make one year. I wanted to be invited to the Pro-Bowl Game and was fortunate enough to play there. I thought that if we could just be the world champions, this would be the achievement of the ultimate goal I had been working for all my life. In 1956 we became world champions. We beat the Chicago Bears 47 to 7. And yet, after reaching this goal, I still found something missing.

I returned to Dallas in 1958 right after we had played Baltimore in the game billed as "the greatest game ever played." We had a sudden-death overtime for the championship, and Baltimore beat us in the last few minutes. After returning to Dallas, a good friend of mine invited me to attend a Bible breakfast being held at 7:30 on Wednesday morning in the Melrose Hotel. Of course I had been to church and Sunday school all my life and had read some of the Bible. I didn't feel that I was morally bad. I had a good conscience. I knew when I did something wrong that it was wrong, and I did feel like I was pretty good from that standpoint. I decided to attend the Bible discussion group, and I remember the first few lessons very clearly. We were studying Genesis, and after reading the text closely I found that the people in the Old Testament were about as bad as we are today. It didn't make a real impression on me.

Later on, after we finished the study of Genesis, we moved on to Matthew in the New Testament. I had heard the stories

39

of the Bible during my early training at the First Methodist Church in Mission. But when we began our study in the New Testament and I had the first opportunity really to study this scripture, I finally discovered what was actually there.

Here I was, thirty-three years old, discovering the contents of a book that had been at my elbow all my life. I started reading such things as, "Therefore, I tell you, do not be anxious about your life, what you shall eat or what you shall drink, nor about your body, what you shall put on. Is not life more than food, and body more than clothing?" And the scripture continued: "Do not be anxious about tomorrow, for tomorrow will be anxious for itself. Let the day's own trouble be sufficient for the day." Again I read, "Ask, and it shall be given you; seek, and you will find; knock, and it will be opened." I kept reading these things over and over. As I read them, and as I studied them, something started to get through to me. Here was something that I had never seen in all the years I had attended church and Sunday school—the real story of the good news that was there in the Bible. I went on to read that "Everyone who hears these words of mine and does them will be like the wise man who built his house upon the rock; and the rain fell, and the floods came, and the winds blew and beat upon that house, but it did not fall, because it had been founded on the rock."

My eyes were finally opened to what it really means to be a Christian. For the first time I recognized the difference between a Christian and a "churchgoer." All my life I had been a churchgoer and not a Christian. For the first time I discovered what Jesus meant when he said, "I came that they may have life and have it more abundantly." My desire to be the best coach in football or to have the Dallas Cowboys eventually get to be the world champions was not curtailed; but it is amazing the different ways I looked at things once

40

Christ came into my life. I looked at my family differently, I looked at my friends differently, I looked at accomplishments differently, and I looked at failures differently. It was really a revelation, and I wish I had the words to express what I felt once I discovered this. No more is there a gnawing feeling in my insides to reach a distant goal. Now I live from day to day, enjoy the accomplishments, and face the failures without the feeling of having my life incomplete. I know that what I was seeking all the time was Jesus Christ.

Life itself is finding the right relationship with Christ. The team was in Miami for the playoff game and we were enjoying ourselves very much before the ball game. We play on Sunday. It is not something we like to do, but our profession requires playing on Sunday. Always, wherever we are, we invite a minister or a layman to come in and talk to us. Our game preparation begins at 9:30 on Sunday morning and this is our only opportunity to have church service. On this particular Sunday a minister came to the hotel and gave us a short lesson. It hit home with me because it was entitled "The Tragedy of a Wasted Life." I will never forget it because it made me think about how much more my life could have meant and how much more enjoyment I might have had had I discovered Jesus Christ when I was a boy. My parents were wonderful. They raised me to know right from wrong, and I had a good homelife; but somewhere along the way I had missed the good news that Christ has to offer.

I hope that in some way I have encouraged someone to seek Jesus Christ. The place to look is in the Bible because that is where the story is. Look in it, read it, study it, and it will change your life—I will guarantee you that. The same story has changed the lives of Raymond Berry, Don Shinnick, "Buddy" Dial, and many of the football players across the country who are looked up to. They are great Christians. We have a number of them on the Cowboy team, as well as on other teams in the N.F.L. Billy Wade, the great quarterback from the Bears, and Fran Tarkenton, quarterback for the Giants, are both active in the Fellowship of Christian Athletes.

Let me say one more thing: Being a Christian doesn't help you win a football game, but it does help you win a more important game—the game of life.

By Ronald Reagan
Governor of California

To many it might seem that the locker room of a professional football team has little to do with "bearing witness," but the gridiron certainly is not off limits to God.

We are great fans of the Los Angeles Rams, as my son Skipper would be the first to tell you. One of his proudest possessions is a Ram T-shirt that was presented to him by Roman Gabriel five years ago.

The shirt became somewhat threadbare and since it was a size 54, was not exactly a perfect fit for a twelve-year-old, but Skipper continued to wear it proudly whenever he watched the Rams' games on television.

Unfortunately we don't often get to the stadium to watch the Rams although in 1969 we were lucky enough to be on the scene when they played the Vikings.

What should have been one of the most exciting days in Skipper's life turned out to be heartbreaking, because his heroes, after eleven straight victories, lost to the Vikings.

The loss of the game, however, wasn't as heartbreaking to him as some of the cynical remarks we heard around us as we sat in the stands.

Some so-called fans complained that "Those guys play for money and they've already won the title so they just went through the motions." One critic even suggested that the team "kind of shaded the points to help the gamblers."

Skipper didn't say much, but I could tell by his expression what he was thinking. I hadn't told him that we were invited to visit the team's locker room after the game and I hoped that being in the same room with his heroes would lift his sagging spirits.

We got to the locker room just as the thundering herd came in. One look at those sweating, bleeding giants should have been enough to dispel any thoughts that they had "just gone through the motions."

Then Deacon Jones, the Rams' all-pro end, charged into the room yelling "Everybody up, everybody up!" The team got up and followed him into what appeared to be a classroom.

Any lingering doubt that the Rams hadn't played their hearts out vanished during the next seven minutes. They blamed themselves for the plays that had gone sour and they expressed self-anger that they had failed to stop the Vikings.

I could tell by Skipper's expression that whatever doubts the remarks in the stands had raised were erased from his mind.

But neither Skipper nor I was quite prepared for what followed. Coach George Allen, who had been listening to the team and talking with them about the mistakes that had been made on the field, stood up.

"All right," he said, "that's enough. Let's give thanks."

His tone of voice made it obvious that what he was proposing was standard operating procedure for the team after a game.

Then, with a father and son standing there watching them, thirty-five football heroes dropped to their knees and recited the Lord's Prayer.

It was a lesson in bearing witness that neither Skipper nor I will ever forget.

Today there are those in our land who tell us God is dead. They ask, "If there is a God, why doesn't he show himself? Why doesn't he offer us proof that he lives?"

We who believe should ask some questions, too.

We should ask questions about the miracle of birth; the miracle of the sunshine and the rain; the miracle of photosynthesis that changes sunlight into energy and makes the plants grow.

We should ask about the miracle of the earth and the miracle of the universe.

And we should ask the ultimate question of all those who say God is dead: "If there is no God, how did all of these things come about?"

It is vitally important that those of us who do believe ask about those who have taken prayer out of the schoolroom and assaulted our spiritual values.

Today we are at a crossroads. We can take the wrong path, or we can dig in our heels and turn to another direction that will result in one of the greatest spiritual revivals of all time.

I am optimistic enough to believe that we will choose the right path.

Over and over again we read the editorials, hear the comments on the talk shows, and listen to the pundits of the airwaves tell us we are not facing up to our unsolved problems.

There are problems—problems of inequality of opportunity, of bigotry and hatred, of racial and religious prejudice. There are the problems of our cities, the problems of poverty and deprivation.

But these same people talk about the complexities of these problems and the great and complex answers that are needed.

I believe, however, that there is a very simple answer to all of these problems. It has been given to us in a pattern of living by the Man of Galilee.

I believe, further, that our halls of government are as sacred as the temples of religion and that every citizen should insist that those who are his servants believe this.

Quite frankly, I don't understand how any man can serve in public office and not rely on God. I don't know how he can possibly bear the burden without God's help. He who tries is just "going through the motions."

MODELS

By Dave Chadwick
Basketball Player University
of North Carolina

As I look back upon my life, I readily see how fortunate I was to have been a minister's son. It seems funny, though, that I did not realize this until very recently. During my childhood and my teen-age years, I did not have a well-rounded comprehension of what it meant to be a Christian. Sure, I went to church every Sunday, but really out of little more than respect for my parents. My entire life revolved around a ball and a basket.

I have been dribbling and shooting a basketball as long as I can remember. By the time I was a sophomore in high school, my body's frame had stretched to six feet, five inches. I began to receive some praise for my ability to play basketball. Naturally, the more praise I received, the more infatuated I became with the game. At the end of my sophomore year, we moved from Kansas City, Kansas, to Orlando, Florida. By then my height was six feet, seven and one-half inches. For the next two years I received any and every honor a young man could want.

With all those honors, I formulated my three d's—determination, dedication, and desire. I modeled my life after Bill Bradley, a man whose dedication to the game reaped him many honors in collegiate and professional ranks. At the end

51

of my senior year I was named to the first team Florida All-State for the second consecutive year. I was finishing up my term as senior class president. At the end of the year, I was named by my fellow classmates as the outstanding senior boy in my class of around 700. The pinnacle of my honors came in late May of 1967 when I signed a full four-year scholarship with the University of North Carolina, then ranked the nation's No. 2 team.

When I entered Carolina, there was no doubt in my mind that I would play. I had a good freshman year, averaging 19 points on a Big Four Championship team that finished 12-4. Going into my sophomore year I was sure that I would get to play. During the summer, I practiced every day to be sure that I would do my best when practice started. From October 15 to December 1, I went through the rigors of preseason practice. When the first game rolled around I found myself sitting on the bench. And that's where I remained for the rest of the season. This was the biggest blow I had ever received. During the next five months I went through the most trying period in my life. I underwent all the frustrations, anxieties, and apprehensions that all young men go through when they are questioning the meaning of life.

The frustration became so great that at one time I considered transferring. I sincerely liked Carolina but I had become so engrossed in basketball that I could not adjust to life when I had the thing I loved most taken away from me.

I left school in May at the end of my sophomore year not knowing if I would return in the fall. Just before leaving school, I was fortunate enough to receive an opportunity to serve on the national college staff of the Fellowship of Christian Athletes. I eagerly accepted. It was during this time that I met such outstanding athletes as Rex Kern of Ohio State and Joe Orduna of Nebraska. Not only these two football players but many other athletes helped show me a quality in their lives that I did not have. They had a relationship with their God through Jesus Christ. It was something that had been said to me hundreds of times in church and in my home but it never had made any sense to me. However, now I saw that there was more in these guys' lives than athletics. It was a unique quality and I wanted it.

When I arrived home in Orlando in late July, with the help of my parents I made a very important decision. I decided to return to Carolina. There were two critical reasons. I realized I could never solve a problem by running away from it, and now there was so much more to my life than basketball.

Strangely enough, I did get to play basketball my junior year. I got to start several games and was a valuable member of an 18-9 ball club that went to the National Invitational Tournament in New York. But it honestly did not matter how much I played. I could have been an All-American or sat on the bench the entire year because in either case I knew God loved me no matter who I was or how much I played in a basketball game.

Just as I modeled my life in basketball after Bill Bradley, I have now modeled my life after Jesus Christ and the way he lived on this earth. I have also reformulated my three d's— determination, dedication, and desire; they always include my Lord. This is my reason for living.

I can now look back and be very grateful for everything that has happened to my life, both glorious and disappointing. For all these happenings have helped me become a stronger and better person, living closer and closer in a day-to-day existence with God. Now I can honestly say that I desire a God-centered existence instead of an ego-centered one. To me, it is real and very worthwhile but only because I am willing to say, "I want Your will, not mine."

APPLIED CHRISTIANITY

By Albert P. Brewer

Former Governor of Alabama

There are those who ask, "Is Christianity at all applicable to us in our affluent society in the year 1972?" I hasten to answer that God is the same Supreme Being who created the world, and he is just as concerned about you and me as he was about the persecutions of Peter and Paul and the stoning of Stephen.

America has long been regarded as a Christian nation and justly so. However, like most Americans, I am distressed over the rising crime rate, drug abuse, juvenile delinquency, and broken homes across the country. "As the twig is bent the tree's inclined." As a parent, I am a staunch advocate of instilling in our children at an early age an awareness of God's love and care. My parents read the Bible to my brothers, my sister, and me and they accorded us the greatest gift parents can bestow—a Christian homelife. Martha and I strive to emulate our parents' example by Bible reading and prayer which have been integral parts of the upbringing of our children. We live this life but once and this is our only opportunity to use our God-endowed talents to serve his kingdom.

In my service in government, as a legislator, as Speaker of the House, and more critically as lieutenant governor and governor, I have faced many difficult problems requiring decisions that only I could make. Yet the making of these decisions affecting the health, safety, and even sometimes the lives of hundreds of thousands of people was beyond the capability of one individual. After receiving the counsel of trusted friends and advisers, I ultimately made decisions relying, to the extent of my ability, upon the infinite wisdom and compassion of an understanding God.

In the depressing, dark days of the last illness of Governor Lurleen Wallace, whose death was to thrust me into the governor's chair, my pastor brought me a placard containing my favorite verses of scripture, "Trust in the Lord with all thine heart; and lean not unto thine own understanding. In all thy ways acknowledge him, and he shall direct thy paths."

This plaque hung on the wall of my office in the state capitol as a constant reminder that there was one place I could always go for advice and guidance.

As a young lad in Decatur, Alabama, the highlight of my day was the time spent waiting at the Louisville and Nashville Railroad depot for the streamliner, "Pan American," to pass by. I was especially excited when college football teams were aboard. But the train passed so quickly. It seemed but a moment until the last car was out of sight. So it is with our lives.

Senator Arthur Vandenberg's all-purpose motto, "And this too shall pass," so adequately describes our short span on earth. In our limited time, we all have many opportunities to witness our faith in word and deed. But so often we do not. I recall reading about a person who lived for forty years in the same block where a church was located. The members of that congregation never once invited him to attend services there. If our lives follow this pattern, we have failed to accomplish a part of life's purpose—revealing our faith to others.

Faith in God has been my mainstay throughout my life, and I cling to this faith for guidance in the life ahead.

A
FREE
GIFT

By Bobby Richardson
New York Yankees (1956-1966)

There is a free gift waiting for you! No, it is not a million dollars, but something much more valuable which has been paid for in full by someone who loves you. It includes peace and joy, no matter what your circumstances, and the promise of eternal life.

In my ten years of playing ball with the New York Yankees I've received numerous letters from people all over the United States concerning the leaflet I wrote entitled "A Purpose in Life." Many commend me for my work with young people, and on being "a fine religious person." Some even add statements such as, "I wish I could be like you but I guess I'm just made differently. I've tried religion and it doesn't work for me."

No, religion doesn't work, and it never will! There are many different religions which people have tried. Some of these are even called "Christian" religions. If I were to lead people to think "religion" or a good life brings peace and eternal life, it would be hypocrisy. All I can truly offer to others is a living Savior, Jesus Christ. Knowing him is a reality, and it is he alone who offers salvation, not any religious system. True Christianity is not escapism, nor a means to gain one's way into heaven by good works, but an involvement with a living person, Jesus Christ. God's word says, "For by grace are ye saved through faith; and that not of yourselves: it is the gift of God: not of works, lest any man should boast."

But the Bible also says that "All have sinned, and come short of the glory of God. . . . All our righteousnesses are as filthy rags. . . . There is none that doeth good, no, not one." I come under this category as much as the murderer, dope addict or front-pew hypocrite. Jesus came to save sinners, and clean-living sinners are just as helpless to save themselves as those who are down-and-outers.

However, the Bible tells us that "[God] hath made him [Christ] to be sin for us, who knew no sin; that we might be made the righteousness of God in him." Paul wrote the foregoing words about God's Son, Jesus Christ, who declared, "I am the way, the truth, and the life: no man cometh unto the Father, but by me." Jesus also said, "I am come that they might have life, and that they might have it more abundantly."

Jesus Christ himself, then, is the free gift waiting for you.

Maybe you have known these things as I did when I was young, but this is not enough. You must have a personal encounter with Christ.

OPTIMISTIC OUTLOOK

By Jack Williams
Governor of Arizona

Abraham Lincoln said that most people are about as happy as they make up their minds to be. Don Quixote found his world of chivalry within his mind; so if each of us believes that which is true, that which is beautiful, and that which is decent and honorable, all the things of kindest vision and fairest myth may suddenly become true!

Such state of mind can chasten our conduct and warm our hearts, because as each believes in his heart, so is he.

The German philosopher Nietsche described a century dominated by dictators unmoved by any moral traditions, plagued by wars made more deadly and devastating by the progress of science, and known as the age of "The death of God."

Some writers would have one believe this describes the world today; but little that is written today is true or will last. This is an age of tinfoil cynicism—chimerical, fantasies of madmen who predict the destruction of everything by evil.

Never have there been so many "Jeremiahs" all so negatively unanimous in declaring that we are destroying the world and the people in it.

In fact, some critics come full circle, protesting that there are too many people in the world, and claiming at the same time that their pollution of air, land, and water will destroy them; all of which is a *non sequitur*. If we have too many people and they are being poisoned off with mercury, lead, and DDT, then we won't have too many people—*quod erat demonstratum!*

In the meantime there is a beauty to enjoy, a job to do, and a challenge to be met.

As after Sodom and Gomorrah a remnant remained, so will some again remain as poets, artists, and dreamers who will tell new stories, paint new pictures, tell of new heroes, chronicle our achievements and possibilities, and we shall be inspired and strengthened. We shall go on and add to our heritage because, as is stated in Ecclesiastes, "Earth will abide." And as Adlai Stevenson once pointed out, "Man will prevail."

So all of us should pray for our own "means of grace" and for our own "hope of glory," purging our hearts of envy, hatred, and malice. We should never suffer the sun to go down upon our wrath, but always go to our rest with peace, charity, and goodwill in our hearts.

SPEAK OUT FOR GOD

By Lester Maddox
Former Governor of Georgia

Some have asked me if I thought it was unusual for a governor or other official in high public office to give his testimony for Christ and to speak regularly in churches. I always answer that if it is unusual, then it is tragic indeed, for it should be the usual thing, rather than unusual, for governors and other elected officials to speak out for God. Nowhere do I find in God's word the teaching that when a person is elected governor, President, or to any other high public office, or when he has received a degree, reached a position of success in business, the professions, or any other field that he is excused from following and serving the Lord.

Recently, a high public official stated that since he had attained that office he was not sure, as a Christian, how he should conduct himself. It is my firm conviction that no Christian should ever question how he should conduct his Christian life in relation to his status, public or private.

The position a man holds should have no bearing upon how he practices his Christian faith. In fact, if he lets that public office, or some other place of prominence, be a determining factor, then he is not the obedient servant God demands him to be. The Christian faith should determine a person's conduct—whether he be high or low in prominence or power.

If I should attempt to adjust my Christian life according to the position I hold, then I would not be living in accordance with God's will and expectation.

I was a Christian long before entering public office, and in my service I have tried to prevent any position of prominence ever becoming my primary consideration or causing me to allow my faith to take second place.

I believe the greater the responsibility a man is given, the greater the need for him to look to God for inspiration, wisdom, and judgment, that he might make the proper decisions.

The Bible records the story of David and Solomon. I like to read this passage because it gives the secret to a successful life. We are told that David said to his son, Solomon, "Be strong therefore, and show thyself a man." David knew that it took a real God-fearing man to be king of Israel, and that God had promised to bless those who would trust in him.

Solomon, upon taking the responsibilities as king, followed the instructions of his father, David, and led his people to obey and serve God. God appeared to Solomon and said, "Ask what I will give you." Solomon did not ask for riches, or power. He said: "I am but a little child; I know not how to go out or come in. And thy servant is in the midst of thy people which thou hast chosen, a great people. . . . Give thy servant therefore an understanding mind to judge thy people, that I may discern between good and evil."

God answered Solomon's prayer and gave him wisdom.

Just as God rewarded Solomon, I believe he will reward any person who tries to follow God's laws and statutes and sincerely seeks God's wisdom. I have kept this in mind as I have sought to carry out the responsibilities of my office. My goals have not been material gains or political power. My purpose has been, and still is, to serve God, my country, and my fellowman. And I have tried to carry out this goal with thanks to God for his love, mercy, and provisions for my needs. I have asked for his forgiveness and for his wisdom that I may perform my task in accordance with his will.

I recognize my shortcomings, and because of this, even though I have not always been the Christian I wanted to be, I keep seeking God's wisdom and direction. My faith in the Lord Jesus Christ and my dependence upon God for strength have meant so much to me that if I lived a million years and devoted all of that time, giving my testimony and directing all my talents and energies for this purpose, I could not begin to repay my debt to God for what he has done for me.

Jesus said, "Ask, and it shall be given you; seek, and ye shall find; knock, and it shall be opened."

I have developed the practice of daily asking of God, seeking his way, and knocking on his door. And the times I have missed the mark, and the times I have failed, have been the times I did not follow this precept.

The Bible tells us, "Let the redeemed of the Lord say so."

As I have had the opportunity to travel throughout Georgia and other parts of our country, I have been proud to tell people what the Lord means to me. I am happy to be a Christian and am not ashamed to stand up and be counted for Christ.

I believe God wants us not only to say that we are redeemed but to live so, and stand ready to die so, if required.

In the Gospel of Matthew, the admonition of Jesus is recorded: "Whosoever therefore shall confess me before men, him will I confess also before my Father which is in heaven. But whosoever shall deny me before men, him will I also deny before my Father which is in heaven."

Jesus said it, and I believe it. I will not deny Jesus before men, and I am confident Jesus will not deny me before God.

So let the world laugh, ridicule, and scorn. I know my God is real. He has sustained me. And although I am the least deserving of all people, he continues to be my hope and strength.

I have never been ashamed to testify for my Lord, and I would not desire to be in any public office—in the governor's office, lieutenant governor's office, legislature, Congress, or even in the White House—if I could not continue to trust in Christ and let the whole world know the reality of my faith.

DECISIONS, DECISIONS

By Robert W. Scott
Governor of North Carolina

Having served as lieutenant governor, and having grown up in a political atmosphere, I thought I knew a little about the office of governor.

But I was not prepared for the feeling that came over me when I took my oath of office. Perhaps it was, as President Truman used to say, knowing that the buck stops here, or knowing that the economy of the state and the well-being of about five million people would be affected in some degree by each decision I made.

For example, I have this feeling when there is a paper on my desk to be signed which may reduce a prisoner's sentence or grant him a pardon. Before signing it, I want to know about his prison record, about his family and his community, and whether they are ready for him to return home. I try to find out if he has a job waiting for him on the outside.

I have the same feeling sometimes when, late at night, or in the predawn hours, I am on the telephone, discussing civil unrest in a community and having to decide whether to call out the Highway Patrol or the National Guard to protect life and property and to restore order.

73

I feel it when a person comes into my office to discuss a problem knowing full well that *that* problem deserves attention and that something should be done about it, but realizing that, in spite of all the prerogative of the office of governor, there is nothing I can do about it.

In times such as these, I find strength in prayer, in asking almighty God for guidance.

It is under such circumstances that I have a full appreciation of my early Christian training—attendance at Sunday school, church services, Sunday evening youth fellowship, and Wednesday night choir practice, my Dad's urging that I recite the catechism, and the fellowship of a Christian rural community whose social life centered around the church.

I believe that every leader in government would acknowledge that he depends upon God, that he is guided in his work by ethical, religious principles.

We may not go out and preach and make a big thing of it. But we have no qualms or shame about it, and we don't care who knows we feel that way.

Those of us who run for public office campaign on many issues. We campaign for programs to upgrade our economy. We advocate more and better roads.

We discuss how we must have more programs to help our physically and mentally handicapped people.

We advocate more parks and recreation areas, and we urge the protection of our environment.

This is all a part of campaigning, a part of politics. Then, when we are elected and take office, we try to implement what we have advocated.

But cannot we also, by our actions and by our deeds, advocate stronger spiritual values?

I have often been asked, as I am sure everyone in public office has been asked, "What are the great moral issues of our time?" I think most people who ask this question are thinking about such things as the death penalty, or liquor-by-the-drink, or the philosophy of separation of church and state, or censoring movies, or the war in Vietnam.

I say that nearly every decision made by a governor, or a President, or a legislator, or a school board member, or any public official is a moral issue. Why? Because that decision affects people.

When a decision affects people, it becomes moral in nature. Somebody somewhere along the line has to decide whether to allocate more funds to employ more custodians in the mental hospitals so that more patients can have better care or whether to allocate more money for more nurses.

Aren't these moral issues? It is not the pay for the individual so much as it is the need to get more personnel to take care of those who cannot take care of themselves.

Or maybe it is a decision on whether to allocate more funds to hire more highway patrolmen, or to buy more traffic lights, or to hire more engineers to design roads and bridges safe for traffic, or to employ more guards in the prisons.

The decisions that I make touch the lives of citizens and affect their well-being. Thus, they are moral issues.

I will be the first to admit that most of us are not conscious of the moral aspects when we make a decision; we do not look upon the decision at the time as being a moral issue. But I think that if we at the decision-making level are Christians, and if we believe in the teachings and principles of Jesus Christ, we act within the moral framework of Christianity whether we are conscious of it or not.

One of the principles on which our nation was founded was that of the separation of church and state. All of us, I think, are in complete accord with the wording in the First

Amendment of the Constitution: "Congress shall make no law respecting an establishment of religion, or prohibiting the free exercise thereof. . . ."

At the same time we who are Christians holding public office can and should relate and apply our Christian faith and our sense of Christian ethics to the political processes and to our decision-making.

If we fail to do this we fail both as Christians and as public servants.

FAITH FOR THESE TIMES

By Walter J. Hickel
Former Secretary of the Interior

Today the United States faces severe tests of its ability to survive as a quality nation. There is much wringing of hands, much fear and despair, much concern about the younger generation.

The way we have been going about attempting to solve our economic and social problems too often lacks the basic ingredients of faith in ourselves, our youth, our institutions.

In such times I hearken to Phillips Brooks, who wrote the words to "O Little Town of Bethlehem" and who expounded this philosophy:

"Do not pray for easy lives—pray to be stronger men. Do not pray for tasks equal to your powers—pray for powers equal to your task."

Beyond our prayers must be faith—a deep, inner feeling that we have done our "homework" and that we have made ourselves capable of meeting whatever challenges and problems lie ahead.

We must believe we will receive what we pray for. That belief has to be so strong, so overpowering, that there is no doubt left in our hearts.

79

Prayer, that strictly personal thing shared only with God, finds its way into the everyday world through the faith that we display among our fellowmen.

Prayer gives us confidence. Faith sustains it. Prayer is a truthful request to God for a solution. As we pray, our faith in God bolsters our optimism that our objectives will be reached—if we do everything reasonably possible in striving for such goals.

Long ago I made a pledge to myself: "Always be truthful." It works. An honest mind, unfettered with extraneous things such as alibis, excuses, and half-truths, functions more rapidly and comes up with workable answers. It has nothing to cloud its clarity.

In prayer, too, we must be absolutely truthful and forthright.

When we measure our faith, let us begin with a belief in our younger people. I refer, of course, to the vast majority of the young. I have faith in that majority—the mature youth who dig in. The immature minority turn to violence and frenzied words when faced with the selfsame problems.

As I told the Student Governments Conference in Washington, D.C., in the fall of 1970:

> "There is nothing to fear if your security lies in your freedom and your principles. Dream big dreams. If you dream little dreams you can only achieve little things. If you dream big dreams, you can achieve the little things *and* the big things."

In short, we must develop faith in ourselves and in God. We should strive always to do the right thing at the right time, not the wrong thing at the right time.

We should not be ashamed to pray. I feel that prayer—honest prayer—is more important now than at any time in the history of our country. It is not a retreat from reality but a regrouping of our moral forces.

A person can be alone with God anytime. There is no specific schedule, no particular place. A prayer is a petition of hope, an honest request for something honest.

I believe that anything we desire can be granted by prayer on one condition: we must believe.

Given that, we cannot fail to attain our goal.

THE DISCIPLINE OF FAITH

By Dr. Ronald W. Roskens
Vice-President of
Kent State University

Faith, at first blush, may appear to be an exceedingly personal factor. Indeed, it is a difficult dimension of life to portray meaningfully to others. Yet, to deny the existence of an indefinable force which sustains one in times of profound personal need seems to me to be absurd.

It is, of course, incumbent upon each one to unravel for himself the mysteries of the Master of the Universe. That God reveals himself variously to man is manifest. But there are many who seem not to have experienced such revelation. Indeed, I have often puzzled over the probable inner turmoil of those who deny the power of a Supreme Being.

For my part, life without faith means virtual absence of inner serenity, of expectation, of hope. Faith eases the agony of personal doubt and despair; indeed, faith anchors one's daily life. It provides, as Professor Elton Trueblood states, "a place to stand."

Whether in a world that yearns for peace that passes all understanding, in a country torn asunder by deepening polarities, or in a university shivering with uneasiness, the discipline of faith is a source of untold strength. Faith, as a starting premise, enables us to hasten the process of reconciliation among and between nations, races, generations, and men.

83

Though he may be armed with all that is knowable, man, nevertheless, is not wholly self-sufficient. In his continuing quest to comprehend the unknowable, man needs the sustaining power of unshakable faith. Surely we must conclude upon examining this question that God is relevant.

GRAB
A
KNEE

By Bill Dooley
University of North Carolina
Football Coach

In 1968 when we faced a giant rebuilding job in football at the University of North Carolina, our team got off to a very disappointing start.

North Carolina State scored twice in the first minute and a half of the season's opener and went on to defeat Carolina by 38-6. The next week, we built up a 27-3 lead against South Carolina, only to collapse in the fourth quarter and lose by 32-27.

Those setbacks would have been enough to finish a lot of teams. But we had a very courageous group of athletes at Carolina that season and they did not quit. They rededicated themselves the next week and vowed to make a better showing in our next game against Vanderbilt at Nashville, Tennessee.

With a tremendous last-quarter comeback, we managed to win the game at Vanderbilt, 8-7. Trailing by 7-0, we scored a touchdown in the final two minutes and then our quarterback, Gayle Bomar, dived into the end zone on the two-point play which won the game.

Our dressing room was a madhouse. The players whooped and yelled and kicked up a real storm. Then, as is customary before and after all of our football games at the University of

North Carolina, I instructed the players to "grab a knee" for a prayer.

I called on Bomar, the quarterback, to say the prayer that night. And I think he spoke one of the most meaningful prayers I have ever heard.

"Dear God," he said, "we thank you for the opportunity to participate in athletics. Guide us safely home tonight. And God, please comfort the Vanderbilt players. They are fine sportsmen and we know the heartbreak they feel at this moment."

Here was a quarterback of a team that had lived with heartbreak praying for the opponent. In his moment of great joy, Bomar did not forget the other football team which had put up such a gallant struggle.

I have heard many prayers in dressing rooms after big football games. In fact, I remember very well the first one I ever heard. It was in New Orleans at the Sugar Bowl when I was a freshman in high school.

My brother, Vince (now the head coach at the University of Georgia), and I decided that year that we were going to see the Sugar Bowl game one way or another. We hitchhiked from our home in Mobile, Alabama, to New Orleans and made it by the day of the big game.

We didn't have tickets, but luckily we were able to get some. Outside the gate at the Sugar Bowl Stadium, a man sold us two tickets for fifty cents apiece.

The game was a thriller, with Tennessee upsetting Maryland, the nation's top-ranked team. Vince and I were so excited at the game's end that we decided to go to the Tennessee dressing room to meet the players.

Somehow, we managed to sneak by the guards at the dressing room door and were walking among the heroes of the Sugar Bowl game. There was a lot of back-slapping and cheering and then, all of a sudden, the room was quiet.

The Tennessee players dropped to their knees and the team captain said a prayer. I bowed my head and listened closely to what the Tennessee captain was saying.

Until that day, I had never seen grown men pray except in church. To me, a prayer was something that little boys said as they knelt by their beds before going to sleep. I was tremendously impressed. Here were the heroes of the Sugar Bowl game kneeling on the dressing room floor and praying to God.

Since I have been a coach, our teams have followed the same practice. We do not pray to win. We do not thank God for victories. We thank him for the opportunity to participate in athletics and for guiding us in our daily lives. We pray also for our opponents as did Gayle Bomar that night in Nashville, Tennessee.

Prayer is a powerful force in the lives of athletes. I saw it for the first time that day in the Tennessee dressing room at the Sugar Bowl. And throughout my coaching career, I have seen the magic that can be worked when a coach says three little words: "Grab a knee."

THE
LAWS
OF LIBERTY

By J. Edgar Hoover
Director, F.B.I. (1935-1972)

Observation and experience tend to bulwark my belief that man is incomplete of himself, that his need of God is overwhelming, and that it is when dependence is placed on his Creator that man most fully realizes his own potential.

Those to whom we are indebted for the priceless gift of liberty recognized this fact. Aware of the immutable laws by which God rules his universe, the founding fathers sought to create a system of government in harmony with those laws. They succeeded astoundingly well. The blueprint for self-rule which they gave the people of the fledgling republic was a remarkable document, yet it very probably would have been ineffectual in any European or Asiatic nation of the time. Why, then, was the Constitution effective as a vehicle of government in the United States of America?

I believe that the answer to the preceding question is encompassed in the utilitarian value of the Christian religion and in what the French observer, De Tocqueville, called Christianity's "conformity to human nature."

Visitors to these shores at our beginnings as a nation found innumerable religious sects proliferating throughout the colonies and on the frontier. They also noted something else in this connection. All sects—and again De Tocqueville

91

spelled it out—"preach the same moral law in the name of God." He found, too, that these numerous sects were "...comprised within the great unity of Christianity, and Christian morality is everywhere the same." No one in early America promoted ideas or activities which might be construed as contrary to Christian morality. Every American seemed to recognize that he must exercise the self-discipline which Christian morality imposes if the great experiment in self-rule were to succeed.

Henry Martyn Field, an American clergyman born in 1822, said flatly:

> "The religion of Christ has made a Republic like ours possible; and the more we have of this religion the better the Republic."

Speaking of the secret of American independence in the last century, Thomas Cipriano de Mosquera, President of the Republic of New Granada, said of the American people, "Religion has made them what they are."

The disciplines encompassed in the Decalogue are essential to personal self-rule. Can anyone conceive of this nation surviving in freedom for any length of time if those disciplines are tossed aside and the moral code—that foundation on which our forefathers reared the rafters of this republic—discarded? What, indeed, "can be done with a people who are their own masters if they are not submissive to the Deity"?

I believe wholeheartedly De Tocqueville was right when he concluded that "Despotism may govern without faith, but liberty cannot." In order to be free, man must live by a moral code. If our free society is to survive, we must repel the attacks on the spiritual beliefs which undergird our freedom. We must resist the forces of materialism which increasingly assail the spiritual bulwarks protecting our freedom.

What of my own belief? I hold with the philosopher in the historical novel that ". . .the spirit is more than meat; that a man, a nation, a millennium grows and is strong, or declines and perishes, in proportion to the spiritual content of each."

We have moved rapidly from a nation rich in the things of the spirit to one rich in material things but one in which many of our citizens are spiritually destitute. The great gift inherent in religion is not being transmitted to great numbers of our younger citizens. The tragic results of our failures in this field are becoming more visible each day in terms of cynicism, nihilism, and anarchism.

I have always believed that the pattern of a man's thoughts and the acts which stem from them necessarily are influenced by his fundamental beliefs—his faith. Indeed, Proverbs tells us that "as he thinketh in his heart, so is he."

I also believe that this free government of ours—this miracle maintained for nearly two hundred years—can exist only as long as man is obedient to God's laws. Man needs God, and, at the end, the long shadow of his life reveals an affirmation of his faith or his denial of it.

Best Wishes
Miss America '71
Phyllis George

A
LOVING
GENERATION

By Phyllis George
Miss America 1971

Is religion out of style? Is it old-fashioned? Is it out of tune with today's life and this generation of young people?

Love is a word tossed about by my "hip" generation. And if we're serious about love, religion can't be out of style! Love of people (our fellowmen), love of country, and love of God is the triangle I believe in. Peace (another often-used word today) and love must come from God—as strength and wisdom come from him.

I am a Christian, but my love can't be a Sunday kind of love, a stopping into a church on Sundays. It's a daily love that comes from a heart that believes. Prayers can be whispered anywhere—at any time—and He will hear them. No, it's not old-fashioned and out-of-style to love God. It's a comfort in today's complicated, sometimes unhappy world.

Speaking personally, I feel very fortunate in my life. Was it luck that I was born to loving parents who taught values in life, and instilled the love of God in their children? Was it luck that I was born with an appearance that happened to appeal to the judges in the Miss America pageant? Was it happenstance that I was blessed with musical talent?

No, it wasn't luck. It was the hand of God. I trusted in him to help guide me during my reign as Miss America, to help me influence other young people to seek his help and guidance.

Young people of today aren't any different than young people of centuries ago. Each generation has fought the "Establishment" in its own way. But each time, the hand of God has guided the young, if they looked for his guidance, and they always grew to be responsible, contributing adults. Is that luck or the wisdom of God?

There are many organized groups that want to destroy our form of government and the society in which we live. The crisis is clear; the challenge is here. We can meet the challenge by *improving* that which has provided so much for so many Americans—not by tearing it down. We can meet the challenge by *strengthening* our government and society—not by dissolving it. As youth of today, we must strive hard to preserve our country and to become well-rounded, productive citizens with an urgent responsibility to God and country.

Jesus talked to young people, guiding them to the solutions of their problems. Today God will help guide us to wise decisions on every important issue. All we need do is let him help us. Perhaps the problems of today loom larger than yesteryear's. Turn to God and he will help.

GOD'S MEN IN BLUE

By Virgil D. Penn, Jr.
Rector's Warden, Episcopal Church
of the Saviour in Philadelphia

Many things are manifestations of faith—the trust of a small child in its mother, the confidence of a pupil in his teacher, a belief in the ideals we live by, in our government and the loyalty of our fellowman.

When we speak of faith, we generally think of a trust in divine and spiritual beliefs. We think of those things which we cannot prove but in our hearts we know are true. We cannot prove that the sun will shine tomorrow, but still we know it will, even though the clouds may obscure it.

One of the greatest faiths that should be exercised more diligently is faith in our fellowman. None of us is perfect. We all have sinned against God and our brother and have been found short in the eyes of the Lord. We heap unjust criticism upon each other without determining the real facts and giving the accused a chance to explain. The Sioux Indians used to make the following prayer: "Great Spirit, help me never to judge another until I have walked two weeks in his moccasins."

My profession is law enforcement. I have the greatest faith in "the men in blue" who dedicate themselves to the American public. These men are the recipients of some of the worse harassment inflicted upon public servants. They endure vocal abuse, are spat upon, and often physically attacked. Many times they pay the supreme sacrifice while trying to make this land a safer place in which to live. Despite all the obstructions and hazards which are thrown into the paths of policemen, the majority of them have faith in the work they are doing. One setback after another seldom dims their desire to accomplish their mission in life.

When a policeman leaves for his day's work, his wife never knows if he will return. She never can tell what may happen to him as he patrols his lonely beat or tours his sector in a patrol car. She also relies on her only support—her faith in almighty God to protect and guide her husband back to his loved ones. I honestly believe this faith surpasses all, especially in the social and moral upheaval that exists in society today.

There is no doubt that some of us policemen had hopes of becoming clergymen. In the Philadelphia Police Department there actually are a few ordained ministers. However, I sincerely believe we can help our fellowmen just as much by being "God's Men in Blue."

MILITARY MINISTRY

By General John D. Ryan
Chief of Staff, U.S. Air Force

Our chaplains in today's Air Force are adding several important new dimensions to their traditional task as they minister to the spiritual needs of our service.

In the traditional pattern, they continue to direct their attention and efforts toward the long-standing concerns of men and women in uniform. This aspect of their ministry is tied directly to the fact that military operations have always imposed heavy demands on the time, energy and ability of the individual serviceman, especially during periods of conflict and international tension.

In these circumstances, the counsel and assistance of the chaplain is often the key underpinning of the moral courage we need to see us through a difficulty of "make-or-break" severity. Over the past several years, for example, the chaplaincy has played a vital role in helping to relieve the many pressures on family life that are brought about by the Vietnam conflict.

These pressures in some cases have resulted from the extended exposure of our people to the hazards and hardships of combat. In other cases they have appeared in the form of bereavement and anxieties arising from reports of our people who are killed, wounded, missing in action, or held as prisoners of war. Without the spiritual resources and moral fiber that our chaplains have helped to nurture within the family unit, these pressures could be unendurable.

As to new dimensions in the role of our chaplains, I have in mind their continuing adaptation to the dynamic and changing conditions that are unique to the Air Force. Our people are operating at the forefront of technological progress and up to the highest skill levels that man has yet attained. And our chaplains are constantly attuning themselves to the new and challenging working conditions of our young blue-suiters in a broad range of flying, technical, and administrative duties. Their frequent visits to the flight line, to our test facilities, and to our maintenance shops will go a long way toward maintaining their firsthand knowledge of "the way things are."

Through this experience, they are gaining a closer insight into the temperament of our young people—their interests, their hopes, and some of their frustrations. The understanding, encouragement, and moral guidance that our chaplains are bringing to these youngsters are certain to be important factors in their future development and achievement.

Regarding the ministry of our Air Force chaplains, I will emphasize a strong conviction that I have held for some time. I believe that, through their efforts to improve the well-being of our people, they are demonstrating the lasting values of respect for and service to others which is a principle of life that is worthy of our best defense.

EXAMINATION

By Allen Saunders
Cartoonist for
"Mary Worth" Comic Strip

There is a much-repeated story about the little grandmother who, when asked why she studied her Bible for hours every day, replied smilingly: "I am cramming for my finals."

At the risk of being considered facetious in dealing with the most serious of all subjects, may I suggest that sitting down to make a statement of one's faith is likewise the taking of an examination, but this one is comparable to spending several hours with an Internal Revenue auditor. There is a strong urge to make the most favorable impression possible, and the concurrent realization that this is a time for uncompromising honesty. We must "tell it like it is."

There are two related but not identical elements in one's creed: religious belief and a personal code of behavior. The esoteric reasoning and dogmatic pronouncements of professional theologians do not, in general, interest me. The cornerstone of my faith, I suppose, is the firm conviction that Jesus Christ walked this earth, gave man the model for a perfect life, and died to tell us that life does not end with death. He is as real to me as any figure in history, more so even than most of those who passed from the scene only yesterday.

107

I must add that my admiration for the apostle Paul, too, is boundless. Without his dogged, dynamic efforts Christianity might never have taken root in the world.

I believe in a Supreme Being, with some reservations about the word "Being." Picturing God in our own image gives us a warm, conforting sense of the known and familiar. However, I am inclined to feel that, as is true of any of the great mysteries, the answer to the question "What is he like?" is beyond the reach of finite minds. But no one can look at a living creature, a tree, or even a snowflake and contend that this is a universe without a plan. And where there is a plan there must be a Planner, be he possessed of a form such as ours or a form which we are unable to comprehend and visualize.

Beyond the written promises given us in the Bible, I find assurance of an afterlife in the fact that nothing perishes in our universe; it only changes form. I cannot believe that the Great Planner would make human life the sole exception and doom it to utter extinction after a split second on the clock of history.

I view the Bible as an inspiring and, for the most part, inspired book. There are parts of it, like the book of Esther, which impress me only as fascinating historical narrative. Yet even these must be studied for the way in which they set the scene for the great message to follow.

I believe in the power of prayer and have seen and experienced proof of it.

Belief can be approached on two levels: simply, or with the probing, questioning mind of the scientist. The scriptures admonish us to be as little children. When doubts arise, as I'm sure they do for most of us, I remind myself that uncountable millions, including the greatest intellects, have believed. And I ask: "Who am I to have the arrogance to differ?"

Perhaps this is what would be called, in today's vernacular, a mental cop-out, but I find it realistic.

On the matter of ethics, may I call upon another person to speak for me? I have known Mary Worth for more than a generation now. She is an embodiment of all the good women it has been my great privilege to know well—my mother, my wife, my sister, and my daughters—and she is very real to me. Fictional characters have a way of reflecting the ideals which their creators admire and, perhaps, strive to emulate. So I fall back on some basics of Mary's personal philosophy. They are brief and simple.

Let us live and serve, appreciating the wonder of the world we have been given, leaving it, hopefully, a tiny bit better than it was when we came into it.

Let us treat every human being as if it were his—and our—last day on earth.

For, as Voltaire put it: "Every man is guilty of all the good he did not do."

MESSAGE

By Nancy Carr
Miss Georgia 1970

Highland Baptist Church in Tullahoma, Tennessee, was the place of the most exciting discovery of my life. Bill Glass was the evangelist for a fall revival there and the simplicity with which he presented the salvation story let me know that, even as a nine-year-old, I needed Christ as my Savior.

The first twelve years of my Christian life were with this in mind, that Christ had saved me. Then it happened—God called me to do something! He called me to a place where I did not want to be, to work with people I did not want to be with, doing a job I did not want to do. God called me to youth work.

To my knowledge, there had never been a female summer youth worker in our town of Columbus, Georgia, and even until the spring quarter of my junior year at Auburn University, I had no intention of being the first! Even so, God saw fit to lead me to Northside Baptist Church for the summer to fill in for a friend who had been appointed as a summer missionary in Washington and Oregon. I had not really been interested in youth work, but a summer trip to the American hospital ship, "HOPE," had been postponed until Christmas, and this particular church was interested in a girl. All this caused me to feel that perhaps God could use me that summer.

111

It was a wonderful summer for me, not just because I loved those young people but because I learned something very special. I spent my summer telling those kids how wonderful it is to have the abundant life God promised in John 10:10.

Suddenly, I realized that I had been missing the boat. I had accepted Christ as my Savior but that summer, with "my kids," I asked him also to be the Lord of my life. He really made the difference and gave me a new kind of peace and happiness.

Returning to school for my senior year, I missed the kids. I missed our fellowship, and I missed our prayer time. One day I was particularly gloomy, because I had just found out that the girl I had been planning to live with while teaching in Atlanta the next year had been offered a wonderful opportunity for graduate work. Although I was excited for my roommate, I was depressed since three months later I would graduate from college, with no job and no roommate. This, I suppose, was the trauma of my lifetime, and it all caught up with me this particular afternoon.

I had scheduled a meeting with a Campus Crusade for Christ staff member at our university, and because of my depression was not very excited about planning for a college life group. In the course of our discussion I mentioned my problem and she shared with me two verses that had meant a great deal to her as she was about to graduate from college. She read from a translation and changed the wording slightly to make Paul's message to the Romans apply even more to my life:

> "So, then, my brothers, because of God's great mercy to us, I make this appeal to you: Offer yourselves as a living sacrifice to God, dedicated to his service and

pleasing to him. This is the true worship that you should offer. Do not conform outwardly to the standards of this world, but let God transform you inwardly by a complete change of your mind. Then you will be able to know the will of God—what is good [for Nancy], and is pleasing to him [to Nancy], and is perfect [for Nancy]."

After she left I prayed, saying, "Lord, I know that you understand my problem about next year. I know that you have a plan for my life. You know I want to trust in your will for me. Lord, please give me patience, and help me to know when you are leading. Thank you for understanding and loving me."

Perhaps it is a coincidence, but that night I received a call about considering reentering the Miss Georgia Pageant. Because of the afternoon's experience, I gave some consideration to the call which otherwise I would have laughed about and forgotten. Again I prayed, "Although I can't imagine how you could use me in this pageant, Lord, please guide me as I try to answer."

I am still amazed at the way doors opened to make it possible for me to participate. I feel very strongly that God has given me a wonderful opportunity to share with young people. My experiences so far have been a wonderful blessing. I'm looking forward to an exciting future and I'm anxious to use it for him.

TEAMED UP WITH GOD

By Richard B. Ogilvie
Governor of Illinois

My living philosophy can be summed up in the words of the apostle James, "Faith without works is dead."

I have tried to live my life according to that scriptural phrase because it means that life, properly lived, can be a continuous prayer to God.

We are put on this earth to use our talents for the glory of God and to serve our fellowman. I have always believed in doing any task, no matter how difficult, to the best of my ability. As long as I do my best, I'm confident I will receive the necessary spiritual support.

But self-discipline is the key to doing anything well. It is essential to a successful Christian life. In fact, it is essential to success in any field.

In my case, the instruction and example of my parents and teachers were a great help in learning this virtue of self-discipline. Participation in competitive sports also played an important part in this regard. The athlete, whether he be in high school or college, must be prepared physically, mentally, and spiritually to cope with the situations which confront him.

In a similar fashion, we are all competitors in the game of life and we must discipline both our minds and our bodies if we are to compete successfully.

115

We must absorb the competitive spirit of the athlete who comes back twice as hard after he has been knocked down. It is not enough to have the will to win. We must be prepared to pay the price of victory by denying ourselves the luxuries and the pampering which soften our bodies and our minds.

This is true, regardless of our station in life, for God has a special job for each of us. Whatever our individual station, we will be judged on our performance in the particular field of endeavor in which we participate.

All of us have the obligation to discharge the duties of our station in life to the best of our ability. Each of us, in addition, has an obligation to be an intelligent participant in the field of public affairs.

For this is the essence—the very lifeblood—of a democracy, and for some of us the duty of public service is even more specific. Those of us who hold public office occupy a position of trust and responsibility in which we must safeguard the confidence of our fellow citizens. A public servant who is a failure is untrue not only to himself but to his God and to his fellowman.

It is often a matter of interest to see how men gravitate into public service. There are many interesting stories in connection with the launching of public careers.

My own case is certainly one in point. I was a self-confident young tank commander feeling very sure of myself when a shell burst over my tank on a battlefield in France during World War II. The next thing I knew, I was flat on my back in a hospital.

For six long months I was hospitalized with plenty of time and a good deal of inclination to examine my life and its purpose.

All of us are prone to take for granted the good health and

the good fortune which are actually gifts of God. But during this hospital stay, I realized that these things were indeed gifts—and that I owed an obligation to the God who had given me my health and my American birthright.

I also came to the conclusion that I owed an obligation to the country in whose defense I had served and for whose preservation many of my fellow soldiers had given their lives.

When I was discharged from the hospital, I began the public career which has brought me to my present station in life. I can tell you that as a public official, I learn day by day that humility is one of our great virtues.

It would be impossible to deal with the complex problems of society which confront many officials—but particularly an official concerned with law enforcement—without the realization that God's grace is indeed the indispensable factor in any progress toward solution of these problems.

Day by day it becomes more apparent that problems would be impossible of solution and temptation impossible of resistance without the divine help which is offered us in abundance. Each day it becomes more apparent also that God expects of us not only prayer but good works as well.

One of the great saints of Christendom advised his followers: "Pray as if everything depended on God, but work as if everything depended on you."

This is my motto in approaching the problems of my public life and of my personal life. I am sure that, while my efforts in both categories will fall far short of perfection, I can count on the spiritual guidance of the Almighty to more than make up for any deficiency as long as I keep trying.

THE LIGHT THAT NEVER FAILS

By David Lawrence
Editor of U.S. News and World Report

Friction today is the outstanding mark on our national life. Group fights group. Race fights race. Creed fights creed. The battle is not always in the open as the poisoned shafts of intolerance and distrust are carried to the inner recesses of everyday life.

Class wars have become commonplace in our times. They have infected our politics as they have poisoned the minds of men who carry responsibilities in our economic life.

Out of this friction, out of this class warfare, hate has become intensified. The sullen thoughts of labor, of capital, of management, of governmental officials—each nurturing the hurt of wounds inflicted by others, each blaming the other as the true source of frustration—only serve to disintegrate rather than integrate the national spirit.

Patiently we wait for abstract justice to solve our ills with a magic wand from somewhere still unrevealed. But justice is no abstraction. It does not come swooping down suddenly, as if from another planet, to correct here and there the mistakes of yesteryears. The world moves on rapidly, giving to each generation the chance to develop its own sense of justice. Nowhere can the key be found to the problem of national unity, be it economic, social, or political, except in the hearts

119

and minds of the individuals who today wield the scepters of power—we of present-day government; we of present-day management in industry; we of present-day leadership of labor, of agriculture, of education, of the press, and of the professions.

At best the span of life is short. Our entrances and our exits on the stage of passing time are controlled by a destiny higher than we with our finite minds are permitted to understand. When the hour approaches for the final curtain, there is no time to look back, or to try things over again, or even to transmit to others the advice of the era which, having discovered its own mistakes, yearns in vain for another chance.

We shall not achieve honesty in government nor honesty in economic struggles nor honesty in the everyday relationships of neighbor to neighbor until we rediscover the Divine Force that unhappily lies dormant in us, only to be awakened when our hectic days are drawing to a close.

More of us must seek from the living God the guidance, the courage, the determination to reveal truth as against untruth, to unmask dishonesty and implant fundamental honesty, to restrain anger and emotion and substitute therefor the inspired and thoughtful processes of reason.

What we need as a national policy in America is a readiness to understand one another, to have regard for one another, to be tolerant of one another, to be helpful to one another. It is not the acquisitive instinct but it is unselfish giving which needs new stimulus. It is not gifts of money that regenerate the human spirit, but gifts of time, of energy, of oneself—gifts that mean a sharing with one's fellowman the precious gold of an honest heart. These are the nuggets that are imbedded in the soul which seeks, in the purest sense, ever to find fulfillment in the current years—now—and not when it is too late.

Thomas Gray spoke eternal truth when he wrote:
> "The boast of heraldry, the pomp of pow'r,
>> And all that beauty, all that wealth e'er gave,
>> Awaits alike th' inevitable hour,
>
> The paths of glory lead but to the grave."

May we, therefore, ask an all-wise God to teach us how to articulate the needs of this fateful period in the world, and to show us through our individual lives, our neighborhood contacts, our group activities, our business pursuits, our party policies, and our governmental actions how we may make those selfsame paths of glory seem in retrospect the true avenues to a better life.

May we approach our Maker in later days, not with sad recollections but with joyous hearts, ready for the "inevitable hour" because we shall have built a nation which will lead the world in intelligence and self-restraint—a nation triumphant over every complexity of social, economic, and political life.

To achieve these objectives, may we, in the precious years that still remain, turn our eyes again and again to the Light that never fails.

THE
STAGE
OF
LIFE

By Connie Lerner
Miss North Carolina 1970

I thank God for this life because I love it. I am proud to be
what I am because it is an art to be human. It is difficult and
it is an honor. To exist is to struggle, to swim against all that
is ugly and unanswerable in life's current. How we as
individuals can blend in with others is really the test of how
much we believe in God's challenge. Along with life, he made
us playwrights, allowing us to create a play that reads as the
script of our lives. We can do almost anything we dream—
with or without other players, with or without laughter, with
or without consideration for the rest of the world.

I thank the Lord for having given me the religious obligation of bearing the message of freedom to all mankind. On
the Passover, for example, I recall that we did not always
enjoy the freedom we do today, and that we must therefore
commit ourselves to the continuing cause of liberation for all
human beings. We must reach across the ocean to our Russian
brothers, Christian and Jewish, who are in darkness. We
cannot forget that there are many who have died in darkness.
I believe that we must promise to bring a new day to those in
the shadows. I believe that to resist tyranny is to obey God,
and that this call must penetrate the Iron Curtain and any

other barriers against enlightenment and acknowledgment of individual rights.

Yet we face a closer enemy—ourselves! To be unjust to ourselves is to invite condemnation from the world. However, I believe that consideration for others is the only means to harmony, or to a balanced existence in a universe only God has the right to weigh. If we are to live together on earth, then we must realize that this respect for ourselves and each other provides the vital elements to balance the scale. Extremism in any direction will upset the stability in living. I am an extremist, however. I am an extremist against extremism. I know that to force one's beliefs on another is a dangerous step, leading to violence and resentment. Yes, I believe in freedom, but too much freedom results in chaos! We must find that medium where peace exists. People today say this is impossible. Man will always lose, then, if he never tries.

It is a fact that the powers of love transcend those of hate. It is a fact that the wise practice love while the foolish feed on hate. It is also a fact that it is harder to love than to hate. It is more difficult to act wisely than to behave effortlessly as a fool.

Within these statements I believe rests man's challenge. Many temptations arise to deter one from pursuing that which one knows is best for him. Why do we smoke when we know we can get sick and maybe die? Why do we eat fatty foods when we know that our hearts will suffer? Why do we hate when we know it brings war? At such times we are behaving like fools, and we are the ones to suffer. If we are not wise in attempting to make something of our lives, life will make nothing of us. What we think is what we are and will become. Our mind—our real God-given treasure—will give back that which we plant in it. With it we have the chance—each of us—to enrich the world whether or not we are rich ourselves. It is as though we each have pens with which to write. At the end of life I would not want my page blank.

As a beauty queen and as an American woman, I have desired to represent the hidden, in-depth reality of beauty that comes from being human. Life for me is like being on stage. I have had to learn to seek the spirit that comes from sharing the stage with other people, and from following the directions of the Producer. My act as Miss North Carolina has ended, but the play still goes on. I have continued to find other sources through which I can fulfill my obligation to myself, to those who need my help, and to God.

This is my challenge, and I welcome it.

| CREDO | By Admiral T.H. Moorer |
| | Chairman, Joint Chiefs of Staff |

I believe in God. And I believe God believes in us as intelligent, responsible individuals, capable of dealing with the world as it is. I believe in seeking divine guidance and assistance to augment the limits of human intelligence and judgment. I do not believe in God as a cure for inertia or apathy.

I believe every person of faith in every generation is challenged to apply the inviolate word of God to his own life in a physical and social environment that bears little resemblance to the day of the prophets, of Christ, or the apostles. The truth, by definition and by its very nature, cannot change, but the world in which we live changes continually. Man's inventiveness and expanding technical knowledge improve the material aspects of life on one hand and create new problems with each new improvement. Social evolution—and revolution—compel us to readjust our relationships with one another and, indeed, between nations. Social morals, reflecting the fluctuations of change, appear increasingly more permissive. Human creeds and philosophies often appear in conflict with scriptural teaching to confuse and mislead the man who seeks simple answers to complex questions.

I believe in the Bible. I believe the guiding principles are there, changeless and everlasting, and all one needs is a determination to find—or someone to help him find—that God and his word are just as applicable to twentieth-century living as they were in those early, simpler days. It is our responsibility to use these principles to meet the needs of our century.

I believe our national purpose stems from our firm belief, as a nation, in the existence of an almighty God. This faith is a distinguishing feature of our form of government which, by constitution, cherishes our individual rights as gifts from God; and I believe it is the purpose of government to protect these rights—not to deny them.

I believe in the worth of every individual—that every individual has rights and responsibilities; that every individual has something to offer for the well-being of the community and all mankind. I believe with Paul that

"God works through different men in different ways, but it is the same God that achieves his purpose through them all. Each man is given his gift by the Spirit that he may make the most of it. One man's gift by the Spirit is to speak with wisdom, another's to speak with knowledge. The same Spirit gives another man faith, to another the ability to heal, and to another the power to do great deeds. The same Spirit gives to another man the gift of preaching the Word of God, to another the ability to discriminate in spiritual matters, to another speech in different tongues and yet to another the power to interpret the tongues. Behind all these gifts is the operation of the same Spirit, who distributes to each individual man, as he wills."

I believe the important questions today are not so much

128

"What's *wrong* with us?" but "What's *right* with us?" "What gifts do we have?" "What use are we making of our gifts?" "Are we giving of ourselves?" I believe a man must answer these questions *to* himself and *for* himself. He must face himself in the mirror each morning and be satisfied with what he sees!

I believe that God is love—and so is man, in essence and in purpose. And I believe that love comes alive in sharing ourselves with one another as God shared himself with us in the person of Jesus. I believe that it is in this love, this sharing, that we find fulfillment, joy, mutual trust, and peace—the peace that finds intelligent men responding to the rights and needs of one another as they respond to the will of God who made love his first commandment and the mark of those who would choose to be his sons.

ONE THING AT A TIME!

By Eddie Albert
Actor

One memorable afternoon in Japan, I learned a lesson for a lifetime.

I met Isamu Noguchi, the American-born Japanese sculptor and designer, when I went to Japan in 1956 to make "The Teahouse of the August Moon." At a time of tension, he gave me some advice which changed my whole life. In honesty, I use and enjoy it today with every breath I take.

The monsoon had caught us, darkening the skies with rain, holding up our picture six weeks. We were fatigued and depressed. I had seen little of the charm and beauty of Japan so, before we left, I asked Noguchi if he would show me something he considered lovely and characteristic, maybe a Zen Buddhist Temple.

I expected this famous artist to reveal a sight special and exotic, something to marvel at. I was disappointed when he took me out in the country from Nara, a small town near Kyoto, and pointed to an old farmhouse. We entered a large bare room. There was no altar and no priest, no Oriental mystery. An incredibly old woman served us tea. I crouched on the hard floor, my knees hurting, as she brought one thing at a time—a bowl, a copper pot, a tray, and so on. We went through the traditional formal ceremonies.

131

"Now shall we appreciate the utensils?" Noguchi asked. An odd remark! But he went on: "The ceremony was to slow you down with one thing at a time. What you must learn is to appreciate the *moment.*"

He picked up a bowl that had been in front of me for half an hour. I had not really looked at it. Now, as Noguchi turned it in his hands, I saw it for the first time. It was delightfully curved, glowing with a rich gold patina. Then Noguchi motioned toward a slim vase containing three delicate flowers, artfully arranged. I had taken them for granted.

"One thing at a time," Noguchi repeated gently. "Appreciate the moment."

My depression vanished. Ever since then, I have found life exhilarating wherever I am, even in times of stress.

It was strange that an American like me had to go to Japan to learn how to live. But I think I appreciate that moment with Noguchi more than any other in my life—except, of course, this wonderful moment of being alive and knowing it right *now.*

WE
MUST WALK
BY FAITH

By Roy A. Taylor
Congressman, State of North Carolina

In today's world of tension with decisions difficult and choices complex, every person needs a belief—a philosophy of life—in order to provide a purpose and a direction to living. A feeling of frustration exists in our nation, and public leaders and individual citizens need to find support and strength from a source bigger than themselves. So often we must "walk by faith, not by sight."

Many of our young people are mixed up in their thinking. It is only through faith and belief in something worthwhile that they are able to keep their balance and move toward definite, sound purposes.

A person needs faith in God, faith in his fellowman, and faith in himself in order to make his life meaningful and to make his best contribution to better community and world conditions.

During my childhood, I was taught by my parents to have faith in God and was taken by them regularly to Sunday school and church. The Bible was read and studied at home and in church. I believe that the Bible is the book of promise, providing a blueprint for unselfish living—living for a cause. It is the only answer to many of today's social and economic problems. Our greatest problems today are in the realm of

135

human relations. The only solution to these problems is found in the teachings of Christ, the Prince of Peace, who taught that it is more blessed to give than to receive, to turn the other cheek, and to be a good Samaritan.

Today, we so often must place faith in our fellowman. I prefer to trust other people—even though I am occasionally deceived—than to live in doubt and suspicion.

Our form of government requires faith in the public officials whom we elect. First, we must elect officials deserving public confidence, and second, exhibit faith in them unless they prove themselves unworthy. When this happens we should make a change.

In order for our churches to remain strong, we must have faith in our religious leaders. No nation can achieve greatness unless its people believe in something that is sound, enduring, and worthwhile.

A person must have faith in himself. To acquire this faith, one must commit himself to purposeful living and must develop a sense of honor.

Certainly we all need the comfort and assurance which come from such a faith as is found in the Twenty-third Psalm: "The Lord is my shepherd, I shall not want. . . ."